LOVE
POTIONS

TITANIA'S BOOK OF ROMANTIC ELIXIRS

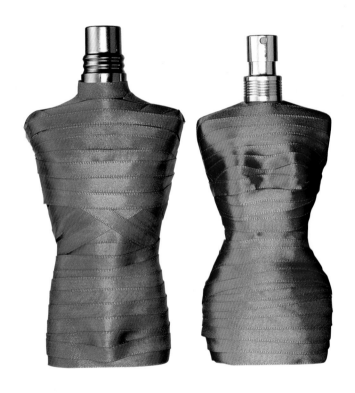

LOVE
POTIONS

TITANIA'S BOOK OF ROMANTIC ELIXIRS

TITANIA HARDIE

PHOTOGRAPHS BY SARA MORRIS

QUADRILLE PUBLISHING

This little volume is especially for Annelise Mary Ebbeck – the goddess of love of my teen years: darling Lisa, where are you now? Also, it is for all those with love in their bosoms: to the witchlings of the world. Keep spreading love and joy and good will, with gentle tolerance for all, and we'll eventually break down centuries of misunderstanding!

'WE'LL TEACH YOU TO DRINK DEEP ERE YOU DEPART!'
Shakespeare: Hamlet

Also by Titania Hardie
HOCUS POCUS: Titania's Book of Spells
BEWITCHED: Titania's Book of Love Spells
TITANIA'S ORAQLE: A Unique Way to Predict Your Future
TITANIA'S WISHING SPELLS: Health, Wealth, Love & Happiness
ENCHANTED: Titania's Book of White Magic
ZILLIONZ: Titania's Book of Numerology
TITANIA'S FORTUNE CARDS
HUBBLE BUBBLE: Titania's Book of Magical Feasts
WHITE MAGIC: Titania's Book of Favourite Spells
TITANIA'S SPELL CARDS: Love & Success, Health & Happiness

An introduction to making love potions *page 6*

Magic Cocktails *page 10*

Mulled Magic *page 34*

Sweet Cordials *page 22*

Body Elixirs *page 46*

Potions to Go *page 70*

Fragrant Rain *page 58*

Appendix *page 82*, Suppliers *page 88*, Index *page 90*, Acknowledgments *page 92*

An introduction to making love potions ♣

Ben Jonson is responsible for the line we all know so well: *'Drink to me only with thine eyes / And I will pledge with mine.'* The allure of erotic behaviour and a potent brew is legendary. This is the simple truth behind a love potion. The erotic brew of heady liquors, imbued with herbal preparations and deliciously scented fruits or flowers, is calculated to alter the state of awareness of the recipient – to relax the nervous, and to excite the bored. Mix someone a love cocktail and you'll be issuing an invitation to see, and be seen, on a wonderfully heightened plateau of senses. ♣ These venerated potions are also chosen for situations which are not specifically romantic: how to create a mood of bliss among guests and relatives you want to work a little happy magic over. There are potions that take you into the bathroom and the bedroom, to sprinkle love-water in your most precious places. The bath products are particularly important, because they ask you to think well of yourself – which is the most bewitching ingredient when you are seeking to find, or improve, a love relationship. ♣ In the pages ahead we include suggestions for the most appropriate vessels and 'props' to accompany your potions: goblets, jugs and carafes, perfume phials, and even 'poison rings', to set the mood and improve the potency of the blends. Some potions are summery, and some perfect for chilly weather. Some are alcoholic, and some tee-total. All will invite the one you love to recapture an essence of romance, and lift your love relationship out of the common place. If you cannot create a significant impact with these precious potions, you must be working on the wrong person. ♣ Remember to pay attention to the aesthetics, and pick pretty flowers, herbs and colours; all of these elements have an impact, and will increase the effectiveness of the spell. If you must make use of dried herbs or flowers – either through seasonal difficulty, or because you have no access to the fresh-grown version – you will still

elicit a good response from these ingredients. See if you can add just a few fresh petals from at least one of the herbs or flowers, just to add potency and visual appeal to the dried ones. ❀ DON'T FORGET, HOWEVER, THAT IT'S QUITE EASY TO GROW MANY HERBS AND SPECIAL LITTLE FLOWERS (LIKE PRIMROSES, LAVENDER AND VIOLETS) IN A GOOD-SIZED POT ON A WINDOW SILL OR A BALCONY. It is always uplifting to use some of your own things in magical recipes, and if you also grow them with love, they have, indeed, added powers and charms in themselves. ❀ SO NOW IT'S TIME TO LEARN A NEW LANGUAGE OF BAR-SKILLS – AND CREATE SOME POWERFULLY POTENT MESSAGES. Create amazing opportunities to use the liquid treats – perhaps by sending forth delightful, hand-written invitations (with scented ink, of course) to a witchy afternoon tea party. Find wonderful china – and have more than one set, so that your mood can dictate the pace. Probably, you'll only want two cups and a pot. ❀ ALWAYS WORK YOUR MAGIC ON PEOPLE WHO ARE FREE TO ACCEPT YOUR LOVING INVITATIONS: DON'T POACH. Witches must be wise and good as well as powerful. ❀ BLESSED BE.

Honouring the self ❀ WE BEGIN WITH A SHORT RITUAL, THOUGH, TO MAKE YOU FEEL POWERFUL, SELF-AWARE, AND FRANKLY, BEWITCHING! Your magic will work better, and your charms have more voltage, if you begin with this very simple recipe for self-confidence. Don't miss it out. ❀ LET THIS RITUAL STAND AS A PRELUDE TO ALL YOUR MAGIC-WORKING AND POTION-MIXING. It is really simple to do, and you will feel a new sense of being in control of your own affairs. Any and all magic works best when you have a calm sense of belief in yourself.

You will need

A small photo of yourself; thin ribbons to embroider with; a small heart-shaped frame, preferably silver; small votive candles, pink or white; a sprig of rosemary; a glass of your favourite wine

❀ WORK ON A FULL, OR NEARLY FULL, MOON. ❀ MAKE A VERY SIMPLE ALTAR AT THE HEARTH OF YOUR HOME, OR IN A QUIET, PRIVATE CORNER, AND DECORATE IT EVERY FEW DAYS WITH SIMPLE FRESH FLOWERS IN COLOURS YOU LIKE. Then, on the evening of a full moon, trim your favourite photo of yourself – taken perhaps at a truly happy moment when you felt terrific – into a small heart shape. Using a wide-eyed darning needle, 'embroider' the edges using very narrow ribbons – either of different colours, or predominantly of pinks, which represent love. You can just do a very simple whip stitch around the edge – or something more elaborate if you like. Make sure you 'caress' yourself mentally – sing, chant sweet thoughts of happiness, imagine sunshine-filled days and all your affairs of the heart being positive. Setting this visual scene is very important, and will do more good to the image you project than you can possibly imagine. ❀ WHEN YOU HAVE COMPLETED YOUR SELF-HONOURING TALISMAN, PUT IT IN A LITTLE FRAME, IDEALLY OF SILVER TO TAP THE RAYS OF THE MOON, AND PLACE IT ON YOUR ALTAR. Light a little candle beside it each day of the lunar month, always seeing your sense of yourself growing. If you have had bad luck before, imagine the waning moon (for the first two weeks after full) cleansing away all the negativity. Then see the growing moon ushering in a time of romance and strong, magnetic personal appeal. From here on in, your luck in love will alter decidedly, and you will feel wonderfully aligned with the powers of the romantic moon. ❀ SO NOW YOU'RE READY FOR A BREW OR TWO...

MAGIC
COCKTAILS

We commence our education in blending brews with the intoxicating kind. Here, we carefully balance alcoholic beverages with a storehouse of herbs and flowers, chosen for their capacity to enhance the endorphin-releasing qualities in the potion – in other words, the ingredients give you a brilliant feel-good factor. The first few are very easy to make, but if you're feeling ambitious and really inclined to master the witchery of potions, put your touch to the last couple, which require a little home-brewing of the alcohol itself: the results will be worth it. Make sure you choose an appropriate recipient – and someone who is free to give you his or her unbridled affection.

Sweet violet wine ❀ THE ANCIENT GREEKS HAD A DEEP RESPECT FOR THE

VIOLET. A symbol of fertility, it was one of the most frequently used ingredients of love potions. Certainly, the properties of the flower make us feel healthy and happy, and also impart a very becoming glow to the skin. Violets also leave a wonderful aftertaste in the mouth, sweetening the breath invitingly. Try this blend with your lover – you'll enjoy the flavour as well.

You will need

125 g fresh violets, or 1 teaspoon dried; 500 g sugar; 3 violet flowers per person, to decorate; 1 bottle very dry white wine

❀ TWO DAYS BEFORE THE POTION IS REQUIRED, PUT YOUR FRESH OR DRIED FLOWERS INTO 500 ML BOILING WATER, AND COVER THE PAN. Leave this mixture to steep for at least 12 hours. The day before the potion is required, strain the liquid into a heavy-bottomed saucepan, and add the sugar. Bring gently to the boil, and then simmer for perhaps an hour at low heat until the mixture becomes quite syrupy. Cool, and pour off into a bottle which you can stopper with a cork. ❀ ON THE DAY YOU WISH TO SERVE YOUR POTION, DIP THE DECORATIVE VIOLETS BRIEFLY INTO THE CORDIAL, SHAKE OFF THE EXCESS LIQUID, AND DUST WITH A LITTLE SUGAR. Allow these to dry for ten minutes; while you wait, put flute-shaped glasses into the freezer, so that when they are taken out they will become deliciously frosty. Now put two teaspoons of violet cordial into each glass, fill with the white wine, and strew the flowers atop the glass. Serve right away, and wait for the temperature to rise.

Summer strawberries ✿ From a purely medicinal point of view,

WILD STRAWBERRIES HAVE A VERY POSITIVE EFFECT ON THE DIGESTIVE SYSTEM AND ALSO FRESHEN THE MOUTH WONDERFULLY. Perhaps for this reason, a meal which is accompanied by strawberry potions is likely to end in a frisky, get-together sort of inclination, rather than leaving you feeling too heavy for passion after eating. However, strawberries are also high in iron and potassium, and may be just the job to inject a little energy into your lover's fatigued spirits. If you think it is tiredness, and the humdrum nature of life, that is preventing you from being amorous with someone, try this.

YOU WILL NEED

A good handful of fresh strawberry leaves, or 1 tablespoon dried; 1 cup white wine;
a good squeeze of lemon juice; 2 teaspoons sugar (optional for taste); 100 g wild or alpine
strawberries, or substitute with a punnet of cultivated ones; 1 bottle good-quality champagne

✿ First make a decoction from the leaves, by boiling them in 500 ml water for about ten minutes quite rapidly, until the liquid reduces to about half. Set aside to cool completely. Strain the liquid into a jug, and pour on the wine, lemon juice, and sugar if desired. Steep this mixture for several hours in the refrigerator – from morning until evening would be excellent. For at least half an hour, chill two glasses in the freezer. ✿ To serve the potion, slice the strawberries in half (or into fine slices, if you're using the commercial variety), put them into the glasses, pour on the chilled mixture, and then top up the glass with the well-chilled champagne. Decorate the edge of the glass with just one strawberry, poised fetchingly over the lip. After a few sips, you should feel a little rush of returning strength and cheered spirits.

Borage and bliss ❀ There is simply no other herb like borage. This

plant has long had a reputation for creating a lovely gentle euphoria, and it is now understood that it does, indeed, stimulate adrenalin and combat depression. If you are lucky enough to be able to grow this beautiful, blue star-flower plant in a pot, or in the garden, it will be the source of many experiments you can make with the flowers as additives to drinks and even cooking. As a potion, the borage cup would be the best choice to encourage a relationship which is flagging, or to push an attraction on to the next stage. You will also find a mulled, winter variant with borage on page 40.

You will need

Juice of 1 lemon; 2 tablespoons honey; 2–3 borage leaves, finely chopped; a few borage flowers, or 2 teaspoons borage tea; 500 ml high alcohol-content white wine (about 13 per cent)

❀ First make a homemade lemonade by adding the lemon juice and honey to 500 ml boiling water, dissolving well, and chilling in the refrigerator. To this mixture, add the leaves and flowers (or tea), and chill for a further hour. An hour before you require the potion, mix the borage 'lemonade' with the strong wine in a carafe and leave to blend and steep in the refrigerator. Strain out the borage leaves, but replace the flowers, and serve in bluish glasses. ❀ The aesthetics and potency will be enhanced if you create some borage ice cubes to float in the glasses. Fill an ice tray with water and put a flower in each compartment. Freeze. These will keep for some time, and can prolong the life of the borage flowers as they come to an end in late autumn.

Alecost brew ✿

THIS IS BASED ON A DELICIOUS-SMELLING, TASTY HERB WHICH HAD BECOME UNFASHIONABLE, BUT IS MAKING A COMEBACK. If you want to order it from a supplier, the Latin name is *Balsamita major*, or sometimes *Tanacetum balsamita.* It is not hard to find if you go to a specialist shop. The common name derives, as you might expect, from its ability to flavour ale or beer; it has a minty flavour which becomes more lemony when it is heated and prepared in food or drinks. Alecost has a very fortifying effect, bringing alertness when imbibed, which makes it the right choice if your beloved is always too tired for amorous adventures. The leaves are often added to pot-pourris to intensify the fragrance of the other herbs. Try it to intensify a relationship.

YOU WILL NEED
15 g dried alecost; 30 ml vodka or kirsch; slices of lemon; a few sugared rose petals, to decorate; a little lemon juice

✿ INFUSE THE HERB IN 250 ML FRESHLY BOILED WATER FOR TEN MINUTES, THEN STRAIN AND CHILL. Make the potion by pouring a shot of vodka or kirsch into a whisky glass, topping with ice and lemon slices, and doubling the volume with the infused alecost (about 60 ml of the liquid). Decorate the glass with rose petals which have been dipped in lemon juice and then dusted with sugar. You now have your beloved's fullest attention. ✿ ACCENTUATE THE 'ALECOST EFFECT' BY ADDING SOME OF THE LEAVES TO YOUR FAVOURITE POT-POURRI (PREFERABLY ONE WHICH IS ROSE- OR CITRUS-BASED), AND PLACING THIS NEAR YOUR SITTING AREA. The smells will make both of you very alert.

Elderflower laughter ❧ This utterly summertime recipe will

DEMAND A LITTLE MORE LABOUR, AS YOU MAKE AN ELDERFLOWER CHAMPAGNE OF YOUR OWN AS
THE BASE. Of course, if you really can't be bothered you can add commercial elderflower cordial to a bottle
of champagne and proceed from there, but it won't be quite the same. The magical content of elder is long
attested – at one time, this tree was associated only with witchcraft – which is why you should handle the
flowers yourself, if possible. The flavour is wonderful, and it is believed that anyone drinking elderflower
in company with a potential lover is apt to feel a very powerful bond for many a long year. Try it and see.

You will need
*10 very large, fully open elderflower 'heads'; 2 litres pure spring water; 250 g sugar; 2 lemons,
sliced; a dash of white wine vinegar; a few violet flowers or lilac florets, to decorate*

❧ MAKE SURE THE ELDERFLOWER HEADS ARE CLEAN AND DRY. Bring the spring water to the boil
in a jam-making pan (or cauldron), remove from the heat, and dissolve the sugar in the water, stirring
constantly. Cover, and set the liquid aside to cool. Only when the liquid is cool should you add the
elderflowers, stirring softly, then add the lemon slices and a dash of white wine vinegar. Cover again and
leave somewhere cool to steep for three days. ❧ STRAIN THE CONTENTS THROUGH A MUSLIN BAG,
THEN POUR THE LIQUOR INTO STERILISED BOTTLES. You will need to cork them carefully – and it
is advisable to wire the corks to prevent the mixture blowing them off. Allow the bottles to stand for
about a week, then chill well. Serve in chilled, frosty goblets, and put a scattering of violets, or lilac
florets, on the top of the vessel. The mixture is quite heady – and will certainly intoxicate the senses.
Do not drive afterwards!

Love potion pudding ✿ This is another recipe that requires

A LITTLE CAULDRON-STIRRING. But it will work deliciously as a pudding if you are trying to encourage someone's feelings for you. The secret is to be completely relaxed yourself, and let the recipe do the hard work for you. Although it takes a little bit of time, it is a perfect option for the potion-maker who is city-bound and cannot get fresh herbs and flowers easily. If you're a supermarket shopper, this is your potion.

You will need

450 g ripe berries in season (such as raspberries, blueberries, blackberries, or red and black currants); 225 g sugar; 1 bottle dessert wine (such as Muscatel, Beaume de Venise, or Sauternes); rose petals or other florets, to decorate

✿ Use a mixture of different berries to get the most potent and delicious effect. Put the different berries, in layers, into clean sterilised jars, and sprinkle a layer of sugar across each layer of fruit as you go. Just before you reach the top of the jar, fill up the contents with the dessert wine. Then cover, seal and store the jars in a cool place. ✿ Let the potion develop for at least a week before dipping into the wickedly wonderful flavours. Serve as a pudding with a good spoonful of Greek yoghurt and a light dusting of raw sugar. Sprinkle rose petals or other florets on top – once again, lilac is a beautiful and sense-intoxicating choice. This has a decided love-potion effect.

SWEET CORDIALS

HERE WE LOOK AT WAYS TO MAKE THE SENSES HEADY WITHOUT INTOXICATION –
so if you're teetotal, or too young to drink, or driving home afterwards, these are the brews
for you. None of them requires alcohol, and they are delicious made entirely without it.
You could, however, add most of the mixtures straight to a glass of champagne or wine if
you wished. Try to get your ingredients fresh: dried herbs and flowers do some of the job,
but they never have quite so much impact as their fresher relations.

True love's brew ✿ ROSES WILL APPEAR AND REAPPEAR ON THESE PAGES.

The idea that roses are 'good for the skin and the soul', as the saying goes, is based on the extraordinary truth that they are the basis of more than 95 per cent of all women's fragrances, and that the petals have long been prized in medicine for cheering the spirits and soothing depression. *Rosa damascena*, in particular, is believed to be good for those who lack love, while *R. centifolia*, the French rose oil base, has a reputation as an aphrodisiac. So find a top-quality purveyor of these magical blooms, and mix your potion.

YOU WILL NEED

Petals from 5–6 fresh flowers of Rosa centifolia *or* R. damascena, *or 20 g dried petals
(from good herbalists); 50 ml honey; sparkling mineral water; extra rose petals, to decorate*

✿ HEAT THE PETALS AND THE HONEY TOGETHER GENTLY AND SIMMER FOR ABOUT TEN MINUTES UNTIL THE HONEY IS COMPLETELY SCENTED WITH THE ROSE. Strain the mixture through a muslin bag, and cool. ✿ TO SERVE A ROMANTIC COCKTAIL, to entice your love to relax and see you in a glowing light while giving you both a sense of well-being, add one tablespoon to a chilled glass, top up with mineral water and stir. Add cubes of ice, and strew with a few petals. Divine!

The primrose tea party ✿ THIS IS A WONDERFUL BREW FOR A

NERVOUS FIRST ENCOUNTER, OR A DATE AFTER AN ARGUMENT. Cowslips and primroses (used usually interchangeably) have a marvellous knack of settling the nerves and arresting a panic attack, and have been used in potions to make the couple more relaxed. They are also a delight to the eye, and taste absolutely heavenly. Try it.

YOU WILL NEED

30 g fresh (preferably) or dried cowslip/primrose flowers; juice of half a lemon; sugar to taste

✿ MAKE A POT OF TEA WITH THE FLOWERS AND ABOUT 750 ML BOILING WATER. Use a teapot with a proper infuser if possible, so that all of the properties of the flowers remain when the tea is strained from within the pot. ✿ JUST BEFORE POURING A CUP, squeeze a little lemon juice into the pot with a small amount of sugar (probably less than a teaspoon, unless you have a very sweet tooth), and serve in pretty cups of sunshine colours – to lift the spirits and calm anxieties. If you can reserve a fresh flower to float in the top, so much the better. Don't forget to place a vase of fresh smelling herbs and flowers on the tea table too.

Heartsease ❁ This uses the beautiful wild pansy (common name heartsease, Latin Viola tricolor) which – along with violet – was one of the most popular additives to the love potions of the ancient Greeks and Romans, and their European descendants. The flower has also been called 'kiss me in the buttery' and 'love lies bleeding'. Besides soothing the spirits, making a wonderful tonic for the heart and blood, and combating the exhaustion of an over-long day, this magical little flower will give a lovely glow to your complexion as you imbibe. An excellent choice for lovers who have become a little jaded.

You will need

Juice of 1 lemon; 2 tablespoons sugar; 75 g wild pansy leaves and flowers – leaves chopped, flowers whole; sparkling mineral or elderflower water, to serve; slice of lemon and 1–2 fresh flowers, to decorate

❁ Make a lemonade by dissolving the lemon and sugar in 500 ml boiling water, stirring well. Set this mixture aside to cool, and meanwhile infuse the pansy leaves and flowers in the liquid. After at least an hour, bring the whole mixture to the boil again very quickly, allowing the boiling to continue for just 30 seconds. Remove from the heat, cool, and eventually chill in the refrigerator.

❁ Serve this potion by straining it into a tall glass half and half with sparkling mineral or elderflower water. Decorate with a slice of lemon and perhaps one or two fresh flowers.

A summer cup ✿ THIS THREE-HERB BLEND IS THE BEST POTION TO USE IF YOU'RE TRYING TO CHEER UP A WHOLE GATHERING OF PEOPLE. Less specific to love, and more to an overall feeling of happiness, mix this little cocktail if you're hosting a family get-together and want to keep the tensions under control. Of course, it's also excellent for cheering up your partner if he or she is a bit low or under too much pressure with work or health.

YOU WILL NEED

15 g fresh marjoram or oregano leaves, or 1 teaspoon dried; 15 g fresh lemon balm leaves, or 1 teaspoon dried; 5 flowers of Rosa gallica *or* Rosa damascena*; 2 tablespoons sugar; juice of 1 lemon, plus some lemon slices; 1 bottle sparkling mineral or soda water*

✿ STEEP ALL THE INGREDIENTS, except the sparkling water, together in a small pan for about one hour, then add just one tablespoon of water to the pan and heat gently for a few minutes. Cool, then pour all the ingredients, without straining, into the bottle of sparkling water. Turn the bottle on end a few times carefully, then place it in the refrigerator and chill thoroughly. Serve through a tea strainer into a glass with crushed ice, and decorate with a few slices of lemon. ✿ IF YOUR GATHERING INCLUDES SOME DRINKERS WHO HAVE NO OBJECTION TO ALCOHOL, ADD A DASH OF VODKA TO THE GLASS AS WELL: it's delicious!

Pink drink ❀ THIS IS REGARDED AS A POTENT FLOWER POTION, because carnations

(which we call 'pinks' when talking about the old-fashioned variety with the strong perfume) were used to spice up wines and foods and were also a symbol of passionate love to the Romans – and to modern Italians. They have a wonderful clove-like taste, but you must use the real thing – called clove pink or clove carnation. Sipping this with someone you like quite well could move the relationship on to a higher plateau.

YOU WILL NEED

1 cinnamon stick; petals from about 6 clove carnations (approx. 100 g fresh flowers);
a pinch of ground ginger; 100 g brown sugar; 500 ml spring water; a few drops of glycerine;
sparkling mineral water or lemonade, to serve

❀ PUT THE FIRST FIVE INGREDIENTS IN A SAUCEPAN AND BRING VERY SLOWLY TO THE BOIL, STIRRING CONTINUOUSLY. Reduce the heat and simmer for about ten minutes; when the syrup begins to thicken, remove from the heat and cool. Add a few drops of glycerine, and the mixture will become pinker. ❀ MAKE UP YOUR POTION BY STRAINING ABOUT 30 ML OF THIS LIQUID INTO A GLASS AND TOPPING UP WITH SPARKLING MINERAL WATER OR LEMONADE. If you're not being teetotal, it is also delicious added to champagne – and will turn it a gentle rose colour.

Moroccan mint tea ✿ THIS IS A LOVELY, SILENT LOVE POTION. It does

not announce its intentions loudly, but quietly offers to conclude a meal with lovely fresh mouths longing
to entangle – adding a touch of energy to carry you both on for a while. Choose this if you want to sneak
up on your loved one and leave him or her with a lingering desire for you.

YOU WILL NEED

*4 sprigs of fresh mint (preferably powerful Moroccan spearmint); 1 tablespoon China or
jasmine tea; 500 ml boiling water; 1 teaspoon sugar; crushed ice*

✿ CRUSH THE MINT INTO A TEAPOT AND ADD THE TEA AND BOILING WATER. Allow the tea
to infuse for about ten minutes, then stir in the sugar. Cool. Serve the tea strained on to crushed ice
in a Moroccan tea glass, decorated with just one or two mint leaves – or if it is a cold night, simply serve
warmed in the tea glasses. The tea will relax you while it promotes sweet breath and a gentle sense
of desire.

A friend of mine – fast becoming a love
diva – places a pot of this tea beside
her bed (with two cups) to wake up to
each morning in cool, mint condition:
she says nothing invites a morning kiss
better than this.

MULLED MAGIC

THESE DELICIOUSLY SCENTED BREWS ARE FOR CHILLY DAYS, when cuddling up and sipping warm drinks by the fire with someone gorgeous is one of the best invitations from the cold weather. Don't wait for the Yuletide festivities to try them out: blend and brew from the end of autumn onwards.

Blackberry brew ✿ Blackberry is a favoured choice for treating

GENERAL FATIGUE, BUT ALSO STIRS THE SPIRITS SENSUALLY. It has a very 'witchy' connection, being a staple ingredient in potions and freely available in hedges. This brew is, incidentally, wonderful for Christmas, but it will warm a cool heart as well.

You will need

1 kg blackberries, from the hedge or commercially grown; 500 g sugar; 25 g whole cloves;
1 cinnamon stick; ½ a nutmeg (kept whole); 250 ml brandy; shreds of cinnamon bark, to serve

✿ CAREFULLY HULL THE BLACKBERRIES, THEN PLACE THEM IN A FOOD PROCESSOR WITH TWO OR THREE TABLESPOONS OF THE SUGAR AND BLEND TO A PULPY PURÉE. Put the purée into a heavy pan with the remaining sugar and the spices, cover, and bring gently to the boil. At the first real bubble reduce to a simmer, and cook for about 20 minutes. Remove from the heat and allow to cool, then add the brandy and stir until well combined. Strain the liquid through a muslin bag into bottles (it will make about 1 litre), and cork. ✿ ALLOW THE BREW TO DEVELOP FOR ABOUT A WEEK, THEN WARM JUST A LITTLE AT A TIME (ONLY AS MUCH AS YOU WISH TO SERVE) OVER SLOW HEAT IN A SAUCEPAN. Serve in shot glasses with a few shreds of cinnamon bark: it should not be steaming hot, but very warming.

Mulled raspberry vodka ❦ Raspberry has powers of rescue:

it is a favourite choice for postnatal women and an excellent all-round winter pick-me-up. Here, it lends its delicious flavour to vodka, and the double effect is one of relaxed well-being. Either use the fruit from the last autumn crop, or buy some commercially.

You will need

250 g fresh raspberries, plus a few to decorate; 25 ml honey; a squeeze of lemon juice; juice of 1 orange; vodka, to serve

❦ Process the raspberries, honey and juices in a blender until very liquid and thick. Push through a sieve, add a little water, and bottle in the refrigerator for a day (it will make about 500 ml).

❦ Just before you serve it on the following day/evening, warm the purée very gently in a pan, and then add just a teaspoon or two to a small shot of vodka, with a raspberry floating on the top (the cocktail should be blood temperature). Take it carefully – for it has a powerful tendency to intoxicate.

Witches' wassail ❧ THIS IS MOST EFFICACIOUS FOR CREATING A LITTLE

GENTLE REVELRY. Borage, which we have already encountered on page 16, is the principal ingredient, and the brew makes a wonderful Yule wassail for getting a whole company of friends into a euphoric state. It will, however, work wonders as well with a solitary admirer.

YOU WILL NEED

Leaves and about a dozen flowers of borage; 50 g cubed pieces of toasted brown bread; 100 g raw sugar; 3 sugar cubes, saturated with Grand Marnier or Cointreau; ½ nutmeg (kept whole); 1 cinnamon stick; a pinch each of ground ginger and cloves; 1 tablespoon orange flower water; a little orange peel; 1 litre stout or brown ale, depending on your taste; 1 litre flower wine (elderflower or bilberry, or mead if available)

❧ MIX ALL THE INGREDIENTS TOGETHER IN A WASSAIL BOWL (A LARGE BOWL FOR PUNCH IS A MODERN EQUIVALENT). Start with the borage leaves, finely diced, and the toast, then add the sugar, the sugar cubes, the spices, the orange flower water and orange peel. Lightly warm the stout and the wine in a large saucepan (not to the boil) and add them to the wassail bowl, a little at a time, stirring well between additions, until the whole mixture is well blended. Finally, scatter the borage flowers over the brew, and allow to stand for about ten minutes until you are ready to serve. It is nice if you can keep it over a low burner, so try to find an appropriate vessel. ❧ BORAGE FLOWERS WELL INTO THE AUTUMN, but if you cannot get borage flowers in the winter, and have none put by from summer days, use some borage tea from a good herbalist and choose another flower for strewing over the bowl at the end. Rose petals or orange peel would also work very well for this.

Wild oats ❀ THE EXPRESSION 'TO SOW YOUR WILD OATS' MIGHT ALMOST BE BASED

ON THE PROPERTY OF OATS TO FORTIFY THE BODY AND RELEASE THE SOUL FROM SADNESS. Saffron, of course, is also an aphrodisiac: so use this in small quantities. So effective can this potion be, that it might be best to warn: HANDLE WITH CARE!

YOU WILL NEED

1 bottle dry white wine; 3 tablespoons dried oats; 1 tablespoon dried oatmeal; pinch of saffron (the real thing, please!); pinch of cinnamon; 1 teaspoon honey; a few gardenia flower petals

❀ HEAT THE WINE VERY GENTLY AND ADD IN ALL THE OTHER INGREDIENTS, STIRRING AS YOU GO. Simmer at very low heat for about ten minutes, then strain through a tea strainer into a two-handled cup, Irish coffee glasses, or punch glasses. Serve just before bed.

This would be extra effective if you sprayed the bed-linen lightly with some cinnamon and gardenia perfume. It will carry the mood deliciously…

Plum for love ❧ THIS IS ONE OF THE MOST POWERFUL AND POTENT HERBAL TONICS, AND CAN BE USED ALL YEAR ROUND, BUT IS PARTICULARLY UPLIFTING IN THE COLDER MONTHS. It centres on plum and rosemary, which treat fatigue and depression; but if you can get the extra herbal tonic powers of the damiana, which acts on the male hormonal system while remedying female anxiety and lack of sexual appetite, it will really add a special element to this absolutely wonderful and true love potion.

YOU WILL NEED

500 g red or purple plums, stoned and sliced; 175 g sugar; 250 ml spring water; 3 good sprigs of rosemary; 10 g citric acid; 18 g powdered damiana, if available (try good herbalists); red or white wine, or champagne, to serve

❧ SIMMER THE PLUMS, SUGAR, WATER AND ROSEMARY IN A LARGE SAUCEPAN FOR ABOUT 15–20 MINUTES, UNTIL SOFT AND FRAGRANT. When cool, process the mixture in a blender, then strain or sieve into a jug and stir in the citric acid. Bottle this if you are going to keep it for a few weeks, or it will last in the jug in the refrigerator, covered with plastic film, for a few days. ❧ BEFORE SERVING, SPRINKLE IN THE DAMIANA (IF USING) AND STIR WELL. Then pour into a glass cordial-style and top with red or white wine (slightly warmed if you like) or even champagne. The recipe will make about 500 ml of cordial, so will last you several days.

Blood red roses ❀ ONE OF MY PERSONAL FAVOURITES, THIS POTION

IS DELICIOUS, WARMING AND SUBTLE, BUT WILL INDUCE GOOD HUMOUR FOR YOU AND YOUR
LOVED ONE. It is also nice to serve to a gathering of friends if they all need a little help with sagging spirits.

YOU WILL NEED

1 tablespoon fresh rosemary flowers; 3 tablespoons fresh red rose petals (with a strong scent);
3 or 4 violet leaves, chopped well; 1 bottle good quality red wine

❀ ALLOW ALL OF THE INGREDIENTS TO STEEP IN THE RED WINE FOR A FEW HOURS IN A WARM
PLACE, THEN STRAIN INTO GENTLY WARMED GOBLETS AND SERVE. If you prefer, you can decant the
wine into a dramatic vessel, after first straining out the greenery.

These ingredients are obviously easiest to find in the summer, yet the brew suits colder, perhaps autumnal days. The solution is to freeze the flowers and violet leaves in a little freezer bag, where they can remain happily for a couple of months, extending your sense of summer. But do try to get some fresh red roses at least for garnish.

BODY
ELIXIRS

Our brains register smell in a very specific way, in the zone next to that which produces the hormones affecting stress and anxiety. Thus perfumes trigger a change in our breathing, and slow us down gently. In this chapter and the next, we look at different potions based on scent, here concentrating on bathing and massage.

Start with a proper ritual for the bath, to get ready for love; then, progress to the art of massage. Using scent, you can send subtle messages to your beloved without having to use words.

Basic body language ✿ SURELY THIS RECIPE NEEDS NO INTRODUCTION?

Massage is the most effective foreplay, since touch releases endorphins (the feel-good chemicals), and these olfactory delights will send your lucky recipient into the realms of bliss. Happily, your nose gets its fair share of pleasure – even if your body is not being pampered. The oils are an expensive investment perhaps, but will go far and last long.

YOU WILL NEED

50 ml almond, or almond and avocado, oil; 5 drops each rose otto and jasmine essential oils;
3 drops neroli essential oil; 2 drops sandalwood essential oil

✿ MAKE THIS BLEND AT LEAST THE NIGHT BEFORE, TO ALLOW THE ESSENTIAL OILS TIME TO STEEP IN THE CARRIER OIL. However, it is also wise to use up the mixture over a week, for the essential oils lose their height of potency after this period unless they are kept cool in their dark bottles. Jasmine invites mystery and stirs the hormones towards sensuality, while rose works on areas of deep memory – promoting a powerful storehouse of future recollections of this sensual moment. ✿ MAKE YOUR MASSAGE STROKES LONG AND UNHURRIED, COMBINING A BASIC LONG STROKE WITH VERY GENTLE KNEADING FOR MUSCLE SPASMS AND GENTLY PLAYFUL PINCHES FOR LOVE. This potion works absolute wonders, so take pleasure in your stroking and do not hurry.

Acceleration tonic ❀ If you think it has been taking too long to move your love affair on to a more powerfully sensual plane, try this rather than the previous, more subtle version. This is less about romance, and more about basic instinct.

You will need

For the female partner: *50 ml almond or olive oil; 4 drops each jasmine and sweet myrtle oils; 3 drops cinnamon oil; 3 drops vanilla essence; 2 drops patchouli oil; pink ribbon*

For the male partner: *50 ml jojoba oil; 3 drops each frankincense, lavender, black pepper and coriander oils; blue ribbon*

❀ Make up each potion, blending the oils the previous day and allowing to steep in pretty little bottles. Tie a pink ribbon around the female bottle, and a blue around the male. Make sure you bring champagne to the massage room, and that both of you are partaking. The smells are really intoxicating, and the feel of the oils on the body will be divine. ❀ The oil is designed to be applied anywhere!

The kiss ✿ THE NEED FOR A DELICIOUSLY INVITING MOUTH CANNOT BE OVER-STATED

– it can turn a partner on faster than any other behavioural language. This mouthwash is designed to be used fresh, and will beat a commercial potion hands down. Pop it into a spritzer for plants, or a perfume atomiser, and top up with its powers after a meal. If the weather is warm, keep it in the refrigerator and quietly apply when you put the last of the cheeses or pudding away.

YOU WILL NEED

125 ml spring water; 6 whole cloves; 1 tablespoon chopped parsley; the zest of 1 orange; 2 tablespoons orange flower water; 2 drops orange essential oil; 1 teaspoon cumin seeds

✿ PUT ALL THE INGREDIENTS INTO THE WATER AND BRING GENTLY TO THE BOIL. The mixture should be cooled, strained, and then stored in a lidded jar in the refrigerator. Shake before each usage, and use about 1 tablespoonful at a time, rinsing completely. This will last up to a week in the refrigerator.

Wake-him-up bath potion ♣ YOU NEED TO INVIGORATE

YOUR SENSES AND THOSE OF YOUR PARTNER IF TIREDNESS OR COMPLAISANCE ARE YOUR BIGGEST ENEMIES TO ROMANCE. This makes a powerfully energising bath or shower gel, and will invite a more enthusiastic approach to the hours ahead. You need not wait for day-break, though. A quick pick-up after the dash home from work is perfect.

YOU WILL NEED

20 ml baby shampoo; 2 teaspoons almond or baby oil; 2 drops bergamot essential oil;
2 drops rosemary essential oil (excites the male libido); 2 drops lemon or orange essential oil;
1 teaspoon witch hazel (to calm the skin)

♣ AGITATE ALL THE INGREDIENTS TOGETHER IN A BOTTLE, THEN WET YOUR SKIN IN THE SHOWER THOROUGHLY BEFORE APPLYING THIS BREEZY MIXTURE ON A SPONGE OR FACE-CLOTH TO THE BODY. If using it in the bath, run under the gushing tap at the beginning, and a little also in the last moment of running the bath to get the prime effect from the oils for inhalation. ♣ THIS MAKES ENOUGH POTION FOR TWO BATHS OR SHOWERS — SO FOR BEST EFFECT, SHARE THE BOTTLE OR THE BATH WITH THAT IMPORTANT SOMEONE! Don't forget the importance of presentation, and choose the best decanters you can find. Hand-write your labels in pretty writing, and tie a sprig of fresh rosemary at the collar of the bottle with a wake-up ribbon in yellow, orange or green, ready for sunny spells.

Enchanted waters bath soak ❀ IF YOUR AIM IS TO MAKE

A FLORAL INVITATION TO BE HUGGED AND PETTED IN A TRULY ROMANTIC WAY, and you need to calm him down and relax rather than pep him up, use this potion instead of the previous one. Remember how famously milk was used by a certain Cleopatra to charm her high-power men.

YOU WILL NEED

25 ml full cream milk; 20 ml scentless (or mildly rose-scented) liquid soap; 4 drops rose essential oil; 4 drops lavender essential oil; 2 tablespoons rosewater; 1 tablespoon fresh rose petals

❀ AGITATE THE INGREDIENTS IN A SMALL BOTTLE, AND ALLOW TO STEEP FOR A FEW MINUTES. Pour the contents into a bath and soak. For best results, tie a pink ribbon around your forehead as you bathe, as this will stimulate thoughts of gentle love. Share your bath, if possible… And don't forget the extra romantic power of a few fresh rose petals or buds scattered at the last on the bath water. Like love in a field of wild roses.

The hair bath ❀ THIS CELEBRATES THE DAYS WHEN FRAGRANT TRESSES

WERE MORE UNUSUAL THAN THEY HAVE BECOME AS A RESULT OF DESIGNER SHAMPOOS. However, there is a special magic woven into these ingredients, and this is the base of a wonderful love spell.

YOU WILL NEED

1 tablespoon ground orris root; 1 tablespoon chopped fresh parsley; 1 tablespoon lavender buds; 50 ml spring water; 4 drops lavender essential oil

❀ BLEND THE INGREDIENTS TOGETHER IN A BOTTLE, THEN STRAIN THROUGH MUSLIN. Shampoo and lightly condition your hair as normal, then apply generously. Do not rinse… Think a spell of enchantment as you work, and watch as you bewitch your lover. **You do not need long tresses for this wondrous witchery. Just behave with full awareness that you have sassy hair. It should be extra shiny and soft to touch, too.**

FRAGRANT
RAIN

HERE WE ARE CONCERNED WITH MAKING PERFUME — FOR OURSELVES AND FOR OUR SPACE. Fragrance is the language of the natural world: from flowers, it is a call to be pollinated, to ensure its futurity through unmitigated attraction. We borrow from their language to create a new one for ourselves – also, essentially, a call to be pollinated.

IT IS IMPORTANT TO PRODUCE A BLEND OF SCENTS THAT WORKS IN UNITY TOGETHER, AND TO MAKE UP THE RIGHT STRENGTH FOR THE JOB YOU WANT TO DO. If you're young and sassy, create one of the 'splash' blends, as this invites closeness because it's not too powerful, but very friendly. If you're older, and your scent needs to linger into the night, choose a 15 per cent blend. Remember, though, that the art of seduction is always in under, rather than over, application.

Elixir of youth ✿ THIS IS A PERFECT POTION FOR THE YOUNG — IN YEARS,

OR AT HEART. It will revive your spirits on a hot, or too long, day, because the scent is light and the combination of geranium and rose eases an overloaded mind. Spritz it onto your body after a shower, and then splash a little over your clothes too.

YOU WILL NEED

3 teaspoons spring water; 3 teaspoons ethyl alcohol (from chemist); 5 drops rose oil; 5 drops bergamot oil; 5 drops rose geranium oil; 1 drop ginger oil

✿ BLEND THE INGREDIENTS IN A SMALL PERFUME BOTTLE, PREFERABLY AN ATOMISER IF YOU HAVE ONE. The mixture will need shaking each time you use it, and makes about 25 ml. This is the ideal brew to entice the opposite sex, without going overboard. It also promotes well-being in the wearer. Sprinkle or spray it lightly on to your sheets and in the curtains to spread the ambience around your dwelling place or office.

I shared this potion years ago with my Sydney neighbour, Zoë, who keeps some in her car to freshen it up too. She works a special magic over everyone who travels with her.

Cream potion ✿ MAKING THIS DELICIOUS CREAM HAS A DUAL PURPOSE, AS

YOU CAN PUT IT ON ANYWHERE FOR THE PLEASURE OF ITS SCENT AND ENRICH YOUR SKIN WHILE
YOU'RE ABOUT IT. In the recipe on page 69, we move this process a step further, and make solid scent.

YOU WILL NEED

*150 g emulsifying ointment (available from good pharmacies); 75 ml glycerine; 10 ml each
of three floral essential oils of your choice (make rose one of them); 10 g ground orris root
(available from good herbalists)*

✿ ORRIS ROOT IS WONDERFUL FOR THE SKIN, AS WELL AS IMPARTING A DELICIOUS FRAGRANCE
AND PROLONGING THE 'LIFE' OF THE OTHER SCENTS. Rose oil is also nourishing for the skin, and
your other two choices should be tested to see if they blend harmoniously. ✿ MELT THE OINTMENT
AND GLYCERINE VERY GENTLY IN A BOWL OVER A PAN OF BOILING WATER (OR IN A BAIN-MARIE),
then add in the oils and orris root and continue to heat for about 15 minutes. Strain through muslin and
cool a little before putting into jars using a broad cookery knife (palette knife), placing cream around the
edges before filling up the centre. ✿ THIS CREAM WILL LAST FOR A FEW MONTHS IF STORED IN
A DARK GLASS JAR AND KEPT COOL. Remember to add a pretty label.

Intimacy ♣ HERE WE TURN UP THE VOLUME: this is the choice if you want to be

absolutely sure you will not be ignored – by a stranger, a complaisant lover, or a tired husband. It is only fair to add that you should be sure you wear this for someone who is entirely free to be enticed by you. It is out of keeping with white magic to have to rename this as someone else's 'marriage breaker'. Be careful!

YOU WILL NEED

4 teaspoons ethyl alcohol; 1 teaspoon spring water; 10 drops tuberose oil; 10 drops rose oil;
6 drops bergamot oil; 6 drops jasmine oil; 4 drops patchouli oil; 4 drops oakmoss oil;
pure pheremone

♣ BLEND ALL THE INGREDIENTS CAREFULLY, EXCEPT THE PHEREMONE, AND PUT INTO A DARK, SMALL PHIAL FOR AT LEAST THREE WEEKS TO MATURE. When you are ready to use it, just dab it on to the wrists and dab one drop of pheremone under the nose. You will exude a potent self-confidence and allure, as well as a feeling of wonderful control.

Pheremone is available at good suppliers (see page 88-89), and though expensive, is a long-term investment which will greatly increase the wearer's sense of well-being – thus making them more magnetic to others!

Potent pourri for marriage ❀ MIX THIS RECIPE FOR A POT

POURRI IF YOU WANT TO PUT GENTLE VIBRATIONS TOWARDS MARRIAGE INTO THE AIR, or to continue the aphrodisiac element after a honeymoon. Place it in the bedroom, and stir each day with your ring finger.

YOU WILL NEED

1 cup each fresh scented rose petals (pink or dark red), tiny roses, rose buds, honeysuckle or jasmine flowers, lavender buds and dried verbena (from good herbalists); 2 tablespoons ground orris root (from good herbalists); 2 drops each rose, jasmine and lavender essential oils

❀ IN A PRETTY BOWL, BLEND ALL THE DRY INGREDIENTS TOGETHER, THEN THE OILS, AND STIR WELL. Cover for a few days with dark plastic to allow the scents to develop – but give the bowl an hour of fresh air each day to avoid the pot pourri turning mouldy. This mixture will now keep for months, but can be replenished in fragrant potency by adding refresher doses of oils when required.

Fall-in-love fragrant pot pourri ❀ This is the best

CHOICE FOR SIMPLY SCENTING THE AIR WITH NOTES OF LOVE. If you want to attract love to a new flat or even in your workplace, this is a subtle but reliable pot pourri mixture. Plunder friends' gardens to get the fresh flowers you need.

YOU WILL NEED

1 cup each fresh violets, sweet peas (mauve and pink for attracting love), scented clove carnations (pinks), sweet woodruff or meadowsweet, and peonies; 1 tablespoon ground orris root (from good herbalists); 2 drops each violet, carnation, sweet pea and peony essential or perfume oils

❀ REMOVE THE PETALS OF THE LARGER FLOWERS AND KEEP SEVERAL WHOLE, SMALLER FLOWERS. Combine all the ingredients in a tightly lidded jar, adding the oils last. Store for four to six weeks in a dry, dark place, agitating the jar at intervals to blend the mixture. ❀ DECANT INTO AN APPROPRIATE VESSEL AND PLACE IN THE HEARTH, ON THE ALTAR OF YOUR HOME, OR RIGHT ON YOUR DESK AT WORK. Bliss for noses and spirits.

Solid scent ❀ THIS IS A WITCHY POTION FOR A FEMME FATALE. It is very evocative and will give you a feeling of magical control at your fingertips as you stroke it on at will. Unlike the cream in the recipe on page 63, which is absorbed into the skin, this one forms a separate layer and will hold the scent well. The best receptacle for it on a daily basis would be a small locket which you could wear around your neck. Be sure to find your aromatic trademark by experimenting with several oils for the right balance.

YOU WILL NEED

15 g white beeswax; 15 g anhydrous lanolin; 60 ml essential oils of your choice (try these groups: bergamot, lemon, neroli, orange; sandalwood, rose, bergamot, jasmine; ylang ylang, clove, vanilla, tuberose; frankincense, petitgrain, bergamot, ginger; rose, myrtle, sandalwood, oakmoss; neroli, lavender, vetiver)

❀ THIS WILL BE A COSTLY FIRST BREW, BUT WILL LAST WELL IF STORED IN THE SAME WAY AS THE CREAM IN THE RECIPE ON PAGE 63. Heat the beeswax and lanolin in a bain-marie (as on page 63), taking care to do this slowly and gently. While it is still warm, pour in your blend of oils (totalling 60 ml: most essential oils come in 10 or 15 ml bottles), and stir well until properly combined. While the mixture is still warm and molten, pour into clean, dark glass jars and label. ❀ WHEN YOU WANT TO TAKE OFF A LITTLE AND PUT IT INTO A LOCKET OR PERFUME RING, USE A WARM KNIFE TO REMOVE IT. Don't let your body temperature make the unguent too soft.

POTIONS TO GO

In our final chapter we mix up some interesting additives for making a potion on the hop – when you simply can't pack the saucepan or the food processor. These simple tonics, powders and cordials are easy to pack in a travel pouch, as it were, and will help you bring a more exciting element to a romantic weekend – or even just an important day at the office. Here is an excuse for some wonderful props: pretty glass perfume phials with good stoppers will come into their own, and can be filled with fascinating, sparkling diamond drops; while tiny lockets, lidded rings, and little blush or powder compacts can take on a whole new lease of life as the accessories of the femme fatale. Take a little shopping spree to find some items that inspire you.

The weekend pillow ✿ TWO SIMPLE ITEMS YOU CAN MIX UP TO

CREATE INSTANT ROMANTIC AMBIENCE AND SENSUALITY, when you are heading off for a weekend of (hopefully) love and passion.

YOU WILL NEED

FOR THE PILLOW POUCHES: *cotton-wool pads; blotting paper; a few drops each of rose, lavender and neroli essential oils; muslin; ribbon*

FOR THE ROOM SPRAY: *3 drops each lavender, grapefruit and lime essential oils; 30 ml spring water*

✿ CUT THE COTTON-WOOL PADS INTO LOVELY SHAPES – MOONS, STARS, HEARTS – AND DO THE SAME WITH THE BLOTTING PAPER. Make a blend of the oils in a small droppered bottle, and put a few drops on to the cotton-wool and paper shapes, allowing them to dry for a few hours in a lidded box. Then put the scented shapes into a pouch made up of muslin, and tied with ribbon. Make two of these (you might prefer to spray your favourite perfume onto the shapes) and put one each inside your pillow slips and those of your love when you're away in a hotel or at a friend's house. Instant bewitchment!
✿ FOR THE SPRAY, agitate the ingredients in a tiny perfume atomiser, then use it around the bathroom and sleeping area to neutralise smells of the previous occupant, add antiseptic reassurance, and create a more familiar and comfortable feel. Your love will soon be very relaxed and purring.

Violet dusting powder ✿ THIS TAKES UP THE MOOD OF SENSUAL

BATHING – AND LEADS ON INTO THE NIGHT. We often forget the sheer sensuous thrill of our body, dusted with translucent powder, which becomes even more silky to the touch than with body lotion. Try this, and you're sure to be a convert. Besides, the scent of you is certain to linger in the imagination… You could also use the bath pouch (see page 76).

> YOU WILL NEED
> *1 tablespoon cornflour or arrowroot powder; 1 teaspoon ground orris root; a few fresh violets or other flower (one choice)*

✿ PLACE ALL THE INGREDIENTS IN A SMALL, TIGHTLY-LIDDED CARDBOARD BOX FOR A FEW DAYS UNTIL THE SMELLS STEEP TOGETHER: then pack them carefully into a small powder compact with a little puff. Dust your upper torso after bathing, and allow the scent to continue into lingerie and even the sheets. This is also easy to apply at the office, between hectic moments, to keep you cool and enticing. ✿ THIS ONE IS AN ABSOLUTE ESSENTIAL FOR A SHORT BREAK IN A SUNNY CLIMATE. It would look divine in a beautiful glass dish, with a few fresh violets added every few days.

Fragrant bath essence ✿ MANY WEEKENDS AWAY ARE CHARACTERISED

BY NICE BATH PRODUCTS IN THE ROOMS – BUT LEAVE NOTHING TO CHANCE. This wonderful bath pouch easily slips into a hold-all, will create a visual as well as scented high for you and your beloved, and should lead quickly to romance.

YOU WILL NEED

30 cm square of muslin; sprigs of fresh rosemary, lavender, pine and lemon balm; a few drops each of rosemary, lavender, pine and lemon balm essential oils; pretty ribbon

✿ MAKE UP A MUSLIN BAG FOR THE BATH WITH THE FRESH INGREDIENTS: rosemary is important for male sensual awareness, and lemon balm for female. Add a few drops of the oils to intensify the smell, and tie the bag securely with a pretty ribbon (pink for love, red or shocking pink for passion, yellow for a pick-me-up). Position the bag underneath the taps, where the water gushes out into the bath, tying the ribbon around the taps to hold it. Prepare this before you go off for a walk, to return to a shared bath before dinner – but set a later hour to eat!

Poudre d'amour ♣ IN DAYS GONE BY, MANY AN ENCHANTRESS HAD A

HINGED RING IN WHICH SHE CARRIED POTENT POWDERS OR EVEN POISON. This sensual powder is a worthy successor to that tradition. See if you can find an antique hinged ring to carry it in, and from which you can subtly dispense a few grains. This exotic powder is ideal for bestowing a serious pick-me-up which tends to playful, erotic friskiness as well. Dish this out to your beloved if passion is simply not on the menu any more. You can take it with you anywhere.

> YOU WILL NEED
> *1 capsule of powdered ginseng; a pinch of powdered damiana; 2 or 3 strands of saffron;*
> *a tiny pinch of ground coriander*

♣ COMBINE THESE FOUR TONIC, APHRODISIAC HERBS CAREFULLY, AND PUT THEM INTO A DRY, STABLE RECEPTACLE. Add them discreetly to a glass of dry cider or ale, and they will soon perk up the imbiber. If you like, scatter a few rosemary or borage flowers in the glass too – for aesthetic reasons as well as tonic effect.

This is a true brew for a femme fatale! See how adventurous you can be in finding ways to utilise its passsionate properties. It even adds a buzz to mineral water: use sparkling rather than still, since the bubbles work faster in the bloodstream.

Moroccan magic elixir ✿ WE BORROW SOME OF THE INGREDIENTS OF THE WARMING AND APHRODISIAC RAS EL HANOUT FROM MOROCCO – OMITTING THE TREACHEROUS SPANISH FLY. If you are cooking for your beloved away from home, try adding this to a lamb stew or a chicken couscous dish. It can also be used in a hot wine. Just carry it with you in a tiny jar: you don't need to use too much.

YOU WILL NEED

A few strands of saffron; ½ teaspoon cumin seeds; a pinch of ground ginger; a handful of tiny rose buds

✿ WARM ALL THE INGREDIENTS TOGETHER VERY LIGHTLY IN A DRY PAN, OR IN THE OVEN, FOR JUST A FEW MOMENTS. Add them to your cooking or, for variation, try steeping them in some warmed red or white wine. Strain the mixture before decanting into a wine jug, and return just a few of the rose buds for decoration. A steamy invitation to a loving evening.

The 'hip' flask ✿ Reinvent the appeal of a hip flask with this excellent recipe of cheeriness for lovers. Perhaps if you are going cycling or walking together, or are just off for a warm weekend of romance, this will get you both in the mood.

You will need

1 teaspoon poppy seeds; 2 teaspoons dried or a handful of fresh jasmine flowers; 2 bay leaves, crumbled; 75 ml brandy .

✿ Steep all the ingredients in a warmed saucepan (but not on the heat), in a warm place, for at least an hour: above the stove, or near some heating, would be ideal. Strain, then decant the liquid into a suitable hip flask. Sip with your beloved at regular intervals over a chilly weekend. Divine!

The perfume garden ✿ THIS APPENDIX IS DESIGNED TO HELP YOU

MAKE CHOICES FOR BLENDING YOUR OWN SCENT. The oils are grouped in families that blend well together, and you can play around to see which ones make up your preferred choice. By understanding the families, you can make a reasonable copy of some 'star' brands. You now also know several techniques for scenting your own talcum powder and bath lotions – so blend away... ✿ YOUR PERFUME WILL TAKE ITS CHARACTER FROM A BLENDING OF HIGH (OR TOP), MIDDLE AND LOW (OR BASE) NOTES – just like music. The middle notes are principally responsible for the true olfactory flavour of the scent, but you should blend from all three groups to get a balanced fragrance. There are some flower perfumes, however, which have perfectly balanced high, middle and low notes of their own: gardenia, tuberose and lovely lavender are amongst these. Indeed, these flowers are often the single-note inspiration for some famous fragrances: tuberose is the key-note of the perfume Chloë, and lily-of-the-valley is the heart of Diorissimo.

The high notes ❧ These vanish fairly quickly, but give the first burst of scent.

Experiment with basil, bergamot, cardamom, coriander, hyacinth, lemon, lemon grass, lime, mint, orange, petitgrain, pine, strawberry and tarragon.

The middle notes ❧ These give your fragrance its characteristic scent, and will last many hours

– usually anything from one to two days. Use the blends with care. You might find it works best to play around one main note, or try to find a floral bouquet. Experiment with black pepper, cypress, galbanum, gardenia, geranium, ginger, honeysuckle, jasmine, lavender, marjoram, mimosa, neroli (orange blossom), nutmeg, peony, rose, rosemary, tea tree, thyme, tuberose, violet and ylang ylang.

The low notes ❧ These have a calming effect, and have the quality of fixing your fragrance.

They will last for a few days, and add a creamy richness to your fragrance. Most are derived from wood oils, and are familiar as incense sticks: benzoin, cedar, cinnamon, frankincense, myrrh, oakmoss, patchouli, sandalwood, vanilla, vetiver.

❧ Always label your blends carefully, noting the number of drops you use. Use a good-quality bottle with a firm stopper, and leave your mixture to steep for a day or two before smelling again to see what you have created.

Scent families ❧ THE FAMILIES OF SCENT YOU WILL BE MOST FAMILIAR WITH

WORK AROUND SEVERAL CENTRAL BOUQUETS. Aldehydes are the most famous floral French fragrances, and they amplify the top notes alongside the middle notes. They are usually floral bouquets, and include the rose and jasmine heart of Joy, which is also present in Chanel No. 5. ❧ THE GREEN FLORALS ARE INSTANTLY IDENTIFIABLE, REMINDING US OF GREEN GRASS AND EARLY SPRING. Vetiver is usually a central note in these bouquets, which include Ivoire (by Balmain), and Armani's Gio. The fruity florals have a high note of strawberry or a base note like vanilla to give the characteristic scent: Elizabeth Arden's Sunflowers, and Calvin Klein's Escape come into this category. Fresh florals centre on citrus, or very light floral notes, and Anaïs Anaïs is a wonderful example; while woody florals amplify the woody base notes: think of Safari by Ralph Lauren, or Lauder's White Linen. The sweet florals are among the most distinctive: Blue Grass (Arden) is the original, and Annick Goutal's Gardenia Passion is a more recent example. ❧ ORIENTALS CAN BE SPICY, BUT THEY CAN ALSO BE QUITE FLOWERY — THE LATTER BEING CALLED 'FLORIENTALS'. If these are your favourites, you are drawn to the voluptuous, musky scents – they are also more aphrodisiac than the lighter florals. The group is typified by Guerlain's Samsara, or Opium (Yves Saint Laurent). The florientals are both powerful and flowery, and mix spices with the flowers: Spellbound by Lauder is a perfect example, as is Joop. The so-called spicy orientals linger more on the base notes of culinary spices: the vanilla-rich Angel (by Mugler) and Comme des Garçons are signature scents in this group. ❧ THERE ARE ALSO FRUITIER ORIENTALS, WHICH COMBINE JASMINE WITH FRUITY NOTES: Casmir, by Chopard, and Laura Biagiotti's Roma illustrate this group. The animal orientals, which have a leathery kind of heart, include Calvin Klein's Obsession, which has amber as a key note; while Donna Karan is also an oriental, but a 'sweet oriental'. ✿ CHYPRES SCENTS EMPHASISE THE LOVELY NOTES OF BERGAMOT AND MOSSY LOW NOTES: YOU CAN SMELL THE RESINS IN THE BASE. Miss Dior and Paloma Picasso's signature fragrance are perfect examples. A more floral chypres – where the floral note is balanced with the undernotes – includes Montana, and a fruity chypres plays on the fruity high notes: Yves Saint Laurent's Champagne is a classic. ✿ IF YOU WANT TO PLAY AROUND WITH THE NEWEST FRAGRANCE FAMILY, YOU MIGHT TRY AN 'OCEANIC' OR 'OZONIC' FRAGRANCE. This is designed to include a fantasy note – of water, or air, or even algae and sea-moss. Base notes are oakmoss, or labdanum, and there is a very light floral overlay. Eau d'Issey is one of the best-known ozonics. ✿ REMEMBER TO APPLY YOUR PERFUME ELIXIR TO YOUR PULSE POINTS, THE BACK OF THE NECK, OR BEHIND THE EARS, FOR MAXIMUM EROTIC EFFECT. Your scent will keep longer in a dark bottle, and you should use up your offerings reasonably quickly: any scent (including commercial scents) has a limited life span once it has been opened.

Tricks to play with your signature scent

♣ Scent lingerie

Use sheets of brown paper and scent lightly with your chosen fragrance. You can also put cotton-wool balls into an underwear drawer, impregnated with a few drops of the oils that characterise your fragrance. To be more aesthetic, use the technique of blotting paper and cotton pads cut into shapes, dipped in scent, tucked into pretty muslin bags and tied with coloured ribbons.

♣ Scent your crowning glory

Nothing is more seductive than fragrant tresses of wonderfully clean hair. Find a glass bottle into which you can decant some good-quality spring water and the recipe for your signature scent – just the main oils. When your hair is still damp from post-conditioning – or just to add style each day – spritz a little of this fragrant water into your hair, and leave to dry as naturally as possible. Perfume is especially effective in the hair, where it lasts longest. Avoid putting neat oils straight on to your scalp, however.

♣ Scent the furniture

Place muslin bags, filled with cotton pads and cotton wool which has been steeped with your favourite scent, behind the big cushions in your lounge, or even into cushions that zip open. When they are leaned upon they will release their special fragrance, and your whole home will start to take on a signature scent of you.

♣ Scent your office

Tie ribbons around files and bunches of pencils, spraying the ribbon first to impregnate it with the smell. Add a cushion to your work chair, and either treat it with a ribbon tied around it (ribbons always add magic and work spells on everyday objects), or fill it with pot pourri and scent. You will offset impersonal smells in the workspace, and soon stamp your own personality on the environment.

❀ SCENT YOUR OWN SOAP

This is often the most expensive luxury to buy, but you can create your own by saturating muslin in your signature scent, and then wrapping the muslin around an unscented cake of soap. Tie it into a dark plastic bag for a few weeks, then you have a delicious bath or hand-basin treat that will send out your bewitching scent everywhere.

❀ SCENT CANDLES

These can be used everywhere. Simply burn a candle for a few minutes until the wax has softened at the top. Blow it out, and then drip in a few drops of your chosen oil/fragrance. Let the wax harden again, and when you light it after a few minutes, it will dispense your fragrance.

❀ BUT NEVER DO ALL OF THE ABOVE AT THE SAME TIME

Overkill is the least seductive thing in the world of scent – as in anything else. Step lightly...

Suppliers

ALEXANDER ESSENTIALS
PO Box 11709,
London SE14 5ZR
Tel: 020 7732 8686
www.alexander-essentials.com
Essential oils and other aromatherapy products including powdered damiana.

THE AROMATIC COMPANY
LINCS Aromatic Ltd,
Unit 18,
Thames Street,
Louth,
Lincs. LN11 7AD
Tel: 0800 996 1148
www.aromatic.co.uk
A wide variety of essential oils.

CULPEPER LTD
Hadstock Road, Linton,
Cambridge CB1 6NJ
Tel: 01223 894054
www.culpeper.com
Dried herbs, pot pourri and oils.

JEKKA HERB FARM
Rose Cottage,
Shellards Lane, Alveston,
Bristol BS35 3SY
Tel: 01454 418878
www.jekka.co.uk
Fresh herbs in pots, and seeds.

KOBASHI ESSENTIAL OILS
2 Fore Street,
Ide, Devon EX2 9RQ
Tel: 01392 217628
www.kobashi.com
A range of essential oils.

MEADOWSWEET OILS
18 Dalston Gardens,
Off Honeypot Lane,
Stanmore,
Middlesex HA7 1BU
Tel: 020 8204 4441
www.meadowsweet.co.uk
A varied range of essential oils.

NEAL'S YARD REMEDIES
Head Office:
26-34 Ingate Place, Battersea
London SW8 3NS
Tel: 020 7498 1686
www.nealsyardremedies.com
Mail Order:
29 John Dalton Street,
Manchester M2 6DS
Tel: 0161 831 7875
A full range of dried herbs and essential oils.

SPACE NK APOTHECARY LTD
Head Office:
200 Great Portland Street,
London WIW 5QG
Tel: 020 7299 4999
www.spacenk.co.uk
Mail Order:
Tel: 0870 169 9999
Pheremone and a range of perfumes.

STAR CHILD
2-4 The High Street,
Glastonbury,
Somerset BA6 9DU
Tel: 01458 834663
www.starchild.co.uk
*Dried herbs, essential and perfume
oils and incense.*

TISSERAND AROMATHERAPY
Newtown Road,
Hove,
East Sussex BN3 7BA
Tel: 01273 325666
www.tisserand.com
A wide range of essential oils.

Index

Acceleration tonic 51
Alecost brew 17
Almond oil:
  acceleration tonic 51
  massage oil 48
Altars, honouring self, 9
Bathing:
  enchanted waters bath soak 54
  fragrant bath essence 76
  the hair bath 57
  wake-him-up bath potion 53
Beer:
  witches' wassail 40
Beeswax, solid scent 69
Bergamot oil:
  elixir of youth 60
  intimacy 64
  wake-him-up bath potion 53
Berries:
  Love potion pudding 21
Black pepper oil:
  acceleration tonic 51
Blackberry brew 36
Blood red roses 45
Body elixirs 46–57
Borage:
  borage and bliss 16
  witches' wassail 40
Brandy:
  blackberry brew 36
  the 'hip' flask 81
Bread:
  witches' wassail 40
Candles, scenting 87

Carnation oil:
  fall-in-love fragrant pot pourri 66
Carnations:
  fall-in-love fragrant pot pourri 66
  pink drink 30
Champagne:
  elderflower laughter 18
  plum for love 42
  summer strawberries 15
Chypres scents 85
Cinnamon:
  blackberry brew 36
  pink drink 30
  witches' wassail 40
Cinnamon oil:
  acceleration tonic 51
Cloves:
  blackberry brew 36
  the kiss 52
Cocktails 10–21
  alecost brew 17
  borage and bliss 16
  elderflower laughter 18
  summer strawberries 15
  sweet violet wine 12
Cordials 22–33
  heartsease 28
  Moroccan mint tea 33
  pink drink 30
  primrose tea party 27
  a summer cup 29
  true love's brew 24
Coriander oil:
  acceleration tonic 51
Cowslips:
  primrose tea party 27
Cream potion 63

Damiana:
  plum for love 42
  poudre d'amour 77
Dusting powder, violet 75
Elderflower laughter 18
Elixir of youth 60
Enchanted waters bath soak 54
Essential oils:
  blending perfumes 82–83
  massage oils 48–51
  solid scent 69
  see also individual types of oil
Fall-in-love fragrant pot pourri 66
Floral scents 84
Flower wine:
  witches' wassail 40
Frankincense:
  acceleration tonic 51
Fruit:
  love potion pudding 21
Furniture, scenting 86
Ginger oil:
  elixir of youth 60
Ginseng, poudre d'amour 77
Grand Marnier:
  witches' wassail 40
Hair:
  the hair bath 57
  scenting 86
Heartsease 28
The 'hip' flask 81
Honey:
  borage and bliss 16
  mulled raspberry vodka 39
  true love's brew 24
Honouring the self 8–9
Intimacy 64

Jasmine:
  the 'hip' flask 81
Jasmine oil:
  acceleration tonic 51
  intimacy 64
  massage oil 48
  potent pourri for marriage 65
Jojoba oil:
  acceleration tonic 51
Kirsch:
  alecost brew 17
The kiss 52
Lavender:
  fragrant bath essence 76
  the hair bath 57
  potent pourri for marriage 65
Lavender oil:
  acceleration tonic 51
  enchanted waters bath soak 54
  room spray 72
  weekend pillow 72
Lemon:
  elderflower laughter 18
  heartsease 28
  primrose tea party 27
Lemon balm:
  a summer cup 29
Lemon oil:
  wake-him-up bath potion 53
Lingerie, scenting 86
Marjoram:
  a summer cup 29
Marriage, potent pourri for 65
Massage oils 48
  acceleration tonic 51
Milk:
  enchanted waters bath soak 54

Mineral water:
heartsease 28
pink drink 30
plum for love 42
a summer cup 29
true love's brew 24
Mint tea, Moroccan 33
Moroccan magic elixir 78
Moroccan mint tea 33
Mulled drinks 34–45
blackberry brew 36
blood red roses 45
plum for love 42
raspberry vodka 39
wild oats 41
witches' wassail 40
Neroli oil:
massage oil 48
weekend pillow 72
Nutmeg:
blackberry brew 36
witches' wassail 40
Oakmoss oil:
intimacy 64
Oats, wild 41
Oceanic scents 85
Offices, scenting 86–87
Oils see Essential oils
Orange flower water:
the kiss 52
witches' wassail 40
Oranges:
mulled raspberry vodka 39
Oregano:
a summer cup 29
Oriental scents 84–85
Orris root:

cream potion 63
dusting powder 75
fall-in-love fragrant pot pourri 66
the hair bath 57
potent pourri for marriage 65
Ozonic scents 85
Pansies:
heartsease 28
Parsley:
the hair bath 57
the kiss 52
Patchouli oil:
acceleration tonic 51
intimacy 64
Peony oil:
fall-in-love fragrant pot pourri 66
Perfumes 58–69
blending 82–83
cream potion 63
elixir of youth 60
intimacy 64
scent families 84–85
signature scents 86–87
solid scent 69
Pheromones:
intimacy 64
Pillow pouches 72
Pink drink 30
Plum for love 42
Poppy seeds:
the 'hip' flask 81
Pot pourri:
fall-in-love fragrant pot pourri 66
potent pourri for marriage 65
Poudre d'amour 77
Primrose tea party 27
Raspberry vodka, mulled 39

Room spray 72
Rose geranium oil:
elixir of youth 60
Rose oil:
cream potion 63
elixir of youth 60
enchanted waters bath soak 54
intimacy 64
massage oil 48
pillow pouches 72
potent pourri for marriage 65
weekend pillow 72
Rosemary:
blood red roses 45
fragrant bath essence 76
Rosemary oil:
wake-him-up bath potion 53
Roses:
blood red roses 45
enchanted waters bath soak 54
Moroccan magic elixir 78
potent pourri for marriage 65
a summer cup 29
true love's brew 24
Saffron:
Moroccan magic elixir 78
poudre d'amour 77
Sandalwood oil:
massage oil 48
Scents see Perfumes
Self, honouring 8–9
Signature scents 86–87
Soap, scenting 87
Solid scent 69
Spearmint:
Moroccan mint tea 33
Strawberries, summer 15

A summer cup 29
Sweet myrtle oil:
acceleration tonic 51
Sweet peas:
fall-in-love fragrant pot pourri 66
Talismans, honouring self 9
Teas:
Moroccan mint tea 33
primrose tea party 27
True love's brew 24
Tuberose oil, intimacy 64
Vanilla essence:
acceleration tonic 51
Violet oil:
fall-in-love fragrant pot pourri 66
Violets:
blood red roses 45
dusting powder 75
elderflower laughter 18
fall-in-love fragrant pot pourri 66
sweet violet wine 12
Vodka:
alecost brew 17
mulled raspberry vodka 39
a summer cup 29
Wake-him-up bath potion 53
Weekend pillow 72
Wild oats 41
Wine:
blood red roses 45
borage and bliss 16
love potion pudding 21
plum for love 42
summer strawberries 15
sweet violet wine 12
wild oats 41
witches' wassail 40

Love Potions

AUTHOR'S ACKNOWLEDGMENTS

Too many to mention: I have learned so much from so many generous-hearted people across the globe.
However, meeting Anthony Dweck at Harrods three years ago has left a wonderful legacy; also Roger Phillips and
Nicky Foy, whose *Herbs* is one of the best reference books of many that I have. Thanks, too, to Candace Bahouth
– a love potion entirely in human form – and her sage husband, Andrew; to Saris and Astrid, who imparted some
ideas along these lines years ago; to Jan de Vries and Lesley Bremness, who know more about herbs, I think, than
anyone breathing; and to the local brewers of lots of herbal tonics in my native Somerset. Special thanks to P, not
just for ideas, and faith in me, but also, very recently, for the gift of African spices she produced for sampling.
To Anne, Jim and Alison, for dedication and professionalism. And if your name belongs here but cannot appear
because of space, yet you know who you are, have thanks from me for so, so much edification and joy. BLESSED BE.

PUBLISHING DIRECTOR Anne Furniss
DESIGN Jim Smith
EDITORIAL ASSISTANT Katie Ginn
PRODUCTION Nancy Roberts

First published in 2002 by Quadrille Publishing Ltd,
Alhambra House, 27-31 Charing Cross Road, London WC2H 0LS

This edition first published in 2005
Reprinted in 2006
10 9 8 7 6 5 4 3

BRITISH LIBRARY CATALOGUING IN PUBLICATION DATA
A catalogue record for this book is available from the British Library

ISBN 978 184400 175 0
Printed and bound in China